Easy Amig

from the series : Sayjai's Amigurumi Crochet Pattern, volume 1

Duckies

p. 14

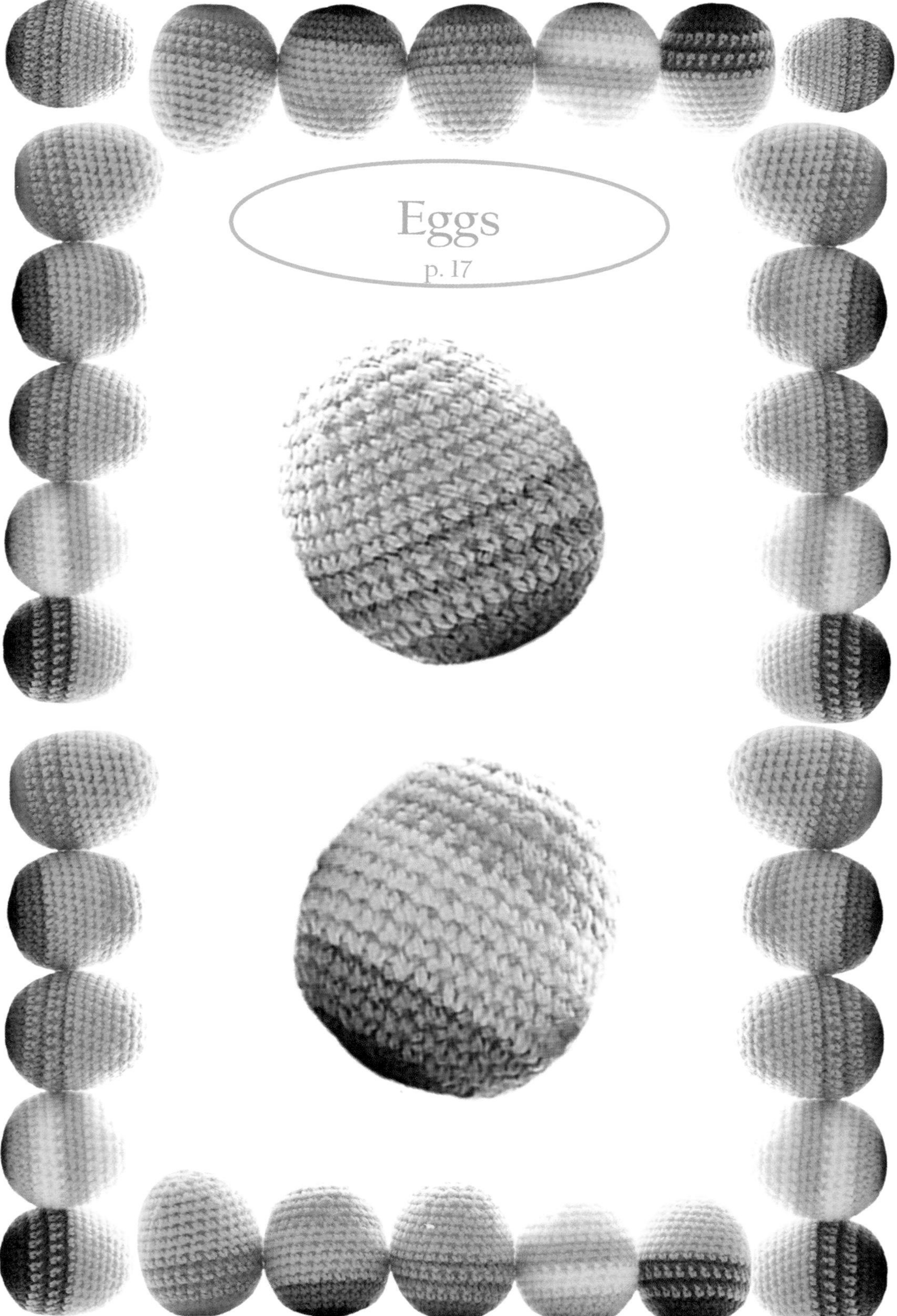
Eggs
p. 17

Little Girls

p. 19

Puffy Pals

p. 25

PIZZA
TEL No.12-345
PIZZA
DELIVERY

Garden Pals

p. 35

Pillow Pals

p. 52

Introduction

Amigurumi is a Japanese word, meaning a stuffed animal toy usually made from crocheted yarn and having an oversized head. Amigurumi is a combination of the Japanese words "ami", meaning crocheted or knitted, and "nuigurumi", meaning stuffed doll.

Easy Amigurumi is a collection of 20 cute small doll patterns and 8 animal pillow patterns. They are very easy to make, using single crochet stitch (UK: double crochet).

Size: The small dolls are 2.4 to 4 inches tall (6 - 10.5 cm). The Pillow Pals are 14 inches high (35 cm).

Abbreviations

This book uses USA crochet terminology.

ch = chain
sc = single crochet
hdc = half double crochet
dc = double crochet
st = stitch
sl = slip
rnd = round
tog = together

Conversion chart for USA / UK crochet abbreviations:

USA Crochet Abbreviations	UK Crochet Abbreviations
sc = single crochet	dc = double crochet
hdc = half double crochet	htr = half treble crochet
dc = double crochet	tr = treble crochet

The size of the doll depends on the size of the crochet hook, the thickness of yarn and how you stuff them; a bigger hook and thicker yarn make a bigger doll. A doll stuffed tightly is bigger than a loose stuffed doll.

You can make the doll smaller or bigger by using different yarn and hook, without changing the pattern.

For the big ducky I used DK (crocheted 2 strands together) and a 5 mm hook.

For the medium sized ducky I used DK (crocheted one strand) and a 4mm hook.

For the smallest ducky I used fine cotton (sport, baby) and a 3 mm hook.

Little Duckies

Materials

These are the materials needed for creating 6 medium sized duckies and 5 eggs.

- DK, Light Worsted (3 Light) Robin DK 15 g each in Pale Pink, Spearmint, Violet, Lavender, Green (Cordial), Peach, Blue (Madonna), Pale Blue, Orange (Jaffa) and Yellow (Sunflower), Cygnet Pato DK 15 g in Pink 912
- 4.00 mm hook (US: G/6, UK: 8)
- Tapestry needle
- 6 pairs of 6 mm safety eyes
- Polyester fiberfill = 110 g

Size

The duckies are 3 inches or 7.5 cm tall. (When you use a 4.00 mm hook and DK/ Light Worsted yarn.)

Remarks

This project is working in continuous rounds, do not join or turn unless otherwise stated. Mark first stitch of each round.

Ducky Colors

Body & Wings Color	Beak & Feet Color
Yellow	Orange
Peach	Orange
Pale Pink	Pink
Spearmint	Green (Cordial)
Pale Blue	Blue (Madonna)
Lavender	Violet

Body

Rnd 1: With Yellow, ch 2, 6 sc in second chain from hook. (6)
Rnd 2: 2 sc in each st around. (12)
Rnd 3: (2 sc in next st, sc in next st) around. (18)
Rnd 4: (Sc in next 2 sts, 2 sc in next st) around. (24)
Rnd 5: (2 sc in next st, sc in next 3 sts) around. (30)
Rnd 6-14: Sc in each st around.
Rnd 15: (Sc next 2 sts tog, sc in next 3 sts) around. (24)

Rnd 16: Sc in each st around.
Rnd 17: (Sc in next 2 sts, sc next 2 sts tog) around. (18)
Rnd 18: (Sc next 2 sts tog, sc in next st) around. (12)

Insert safety eyes 6 sts apart between rnds 14-15 of body then stuff tightly.

Rnd 19: Sc next 2 sts tog around. (6)
Rnd 20: For hair on top; ch 4, sc in second chain from hook, sc in next 2 chs, sc in next st, ch 6, sc in second chain from hook, sc in next 4 chs, sc in next st, ch 3, sc in second chain from hook, sc in next ch, sc in next st, sl st in next st, Fasten off. Sew opening close.

Diagram for Hair on Top

```
          O
          XO
          XO  O
      O   XO  XO
      XO  XO  XO
      XO  XO  XO  <= Rnd 20 starts here
   _X    X    X
XXXX    X    X   <= Rnd 19
```

x = sc
o = chain
_ = sl st

Feet

Make 2

Rnd 1: With Orange, ch 3, sc in second chain from hook, 3 sc in next ch; working in remaining loops on opposite side of chain, 2 sc in next ch. (6)

```
 XXO
XOOX
 XX
```

x = sc   o = chain

Rnd 2: 2 sc in each st around. (12)
Rnd 3-4: Sc in each st around. (12)
Rnd 5: Sc next 2 sts tog around. (6)
Rnd 6: Sc next 2 sts tog around, sl st in first st, leave long end for sewing, fasten off. (3)

Sew rnds 5-6 of feet together, see pictures.

Duck Beak

Rnd 1: With Orange, ch 3, sc in second chain from hook, 3 sc in next ch; working in remaining loops on opposite side of chain, 2 sc in next ch. (6)

```
 XXO
XOOX
 XX
```

x = sc   o = chain

Rnd 2: (2 sc in next st, sc in next st) 3 times, sl st in first st. leave long end for sewing, fasten off. (9)

Sew the opening close. (See photos of the beak below.)

Wing

Make 2.

Rnd 1: With Yellow, ch 2, 4 sc in second chain from hook. (4)

Rnd 2: (2 sc in next st, sc in next st) 2 times. (6)

Rnd 3: (2 sc in next st, sc in next 2 sts) around. (8)

Rnd 4: Sc in each st around.

Rnd 5: Sc in each st around, sl st in first st, leave long end for sewing, fasten off.

Finishing

Sew feet on bottom of body. Sew beak on rnd 14 between eyes. Sew wings on rnd 13 of body.

Eggs

These Eggs are part of the Little Duckies pattern: use the same yarn (see page 14) and a 4.00 mm hook (US: G/6, UK: 8). This project is working in continuous rounds, do not join or turn unless otherwise stated. Mark first stitch of each round.

Size

The eggs are 3 inches tall (7.5 cm).

All eggs are made with the same pattern. Only the colors are different. See which color to use in each round in the tables.

Egg 1 Colors

Egg 1	Rounds 1-5,7,9	Rounds 6,8,10-19
Violet & Yellow	Violet	Yellow
Pink & Blue	Blue (Madonna)	Pink
Green & Orange	Orange	Green (Cordial)

Egg 2 Colors

Egg 2	Dark Colored Egg	Light Colored Egg
Rnds 1-3	Violet	Lavender
Rnds 4-6	Blue (Madon-na)	Pale Blue
Rnds 7-9	Green (Cordial)	Spearmint
Rnds 10-12	Yellow	Yellow
Rnds 13-15	Orange	Peach
Rnds 16-19	Pink	Pale Pink

Egg Pattern

The colors below are for the 2nd dark colored egg. For the other eggs see the colors in the tables.

Rnd 1: With Violet, ch 2, 6 sc in second chain from hook. (6)
Rnd 2: 2 sc in each st around. (12)
Rnd 3: (2 sc in next st, sc in next st) around, changing to Blue in last two loops of last st. (18)
Rnd 4: (Sc in next 2 sts, 2 sc in next st) around. (24)
Rnd 5: (2 sc in next st, sc in next 3 sts) around. (30)
Rnd 6: Sc in each st around, changing to Green in last two loops of last st.
Rnd 7-8: Sc in each st around.
Rnd 9: Sc in each st around, changing to Yellow in last two loops of last st.
Rnd 10-11: Sc in each st around.
Rnd 12: Sc in each st around, changing to Orange in last two loops of last st.
Rnd 13-14: Sc in each st around.
Rnd 15: (Sc next 2 sts tog, sc in next 3 sts) around changing to Pink in last two loops of last st. (24)
Rnd 16: Sc in each st around.
Rnd 17: (Sc in next 2 sts, sc next 2 sts tog) around. (18)
Rnd 18: (Sc next 2 sts tog, sc in next st) around. Stuff. (12)
Rnd 19: Sc next 2 sts tog around, sl st in next st, Fasten off. Sew opening close. (6)

Little Girls

Materials

- Sport, 4 ply yarn (Color: Cream, Green, Light Blue, Red, White, Yellow, Orange, Pink, Purple and Brown)
- 3.00 mm hook
- Black embroidery floss
- Polyester fiberfill
- Twelve 4 mm black beads for eyes or other eyes as desired
- Twelve 4 mm white beads (for decorating flowers)
- Tapestry needle
- Sewing needle and thread for attaching eyes and beads

Size

The Little Girls are 4 inches/ 10.5 cm high.

Remarks

- This project is working in continuous rounds, do not join or turn unless otherwise stated. Mark first stitch of each round.
- All Little Girls have the same basic pattern; Legs, Arms, Head & Body, Hair and Flower.
- Make the dolls by crocheting the legs first then join them together. After connecting the legs, you crochet up for the body and then the head.

Leg

Make 2.

Rnd 1: With Cream, ch 2, 6 sc in second chain from hook. (6)

Rnd 2: (Sc in next st, 2 sc in next st) around. (9)

Rnd 3-5: Sc in each st around.

For first leg, join with sl st in first st. Fasten off.
For second leg, do not sl st in first st. Do not fasten off.

Head and Body

Rnd 1: Hold legs together with upper inner thighs together. Insert hook in the center on innermost thigh of first leg, pull out the loop from second leg, sc in same st (do not count this st just for connecting legs together), sc in next 8 sts on second leg (mark first st), sc in next 8 sts on first leg. (16)

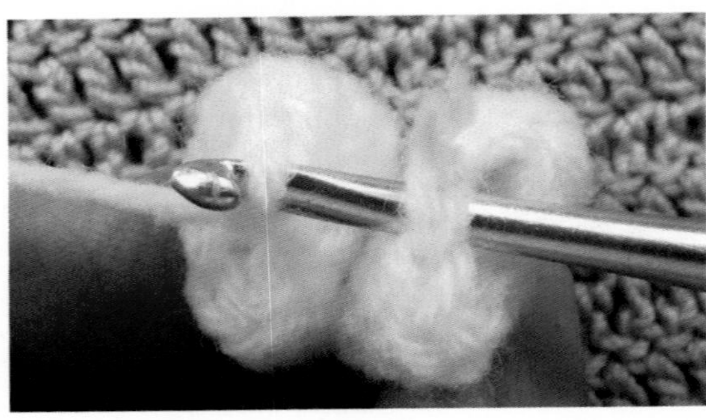

This diagram is showing how to connect the legs together:

The sc is for connecting legs together and go through both legs. The next sc only go through second leg then go round.

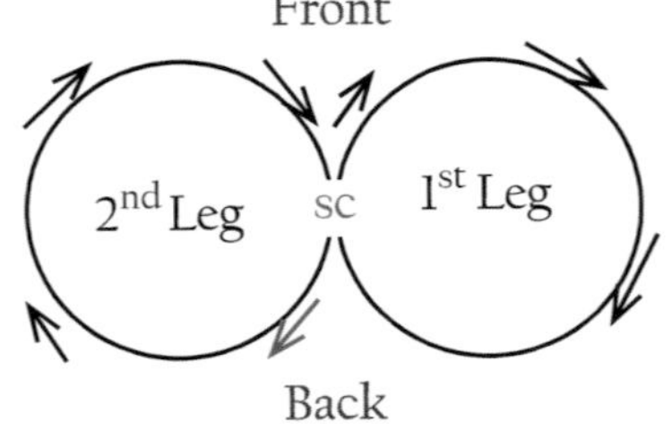

Rnd 2: Sc in next 4 sts, 2 sc in next st, sc in next 7 sts, 2 sc in next st, sc in next 3 sts. (18)
Rnd 3: (Sc in next 2 sts, 2 sc in next st) around. Stuff. (24)
Rnd 4: Sc in next 2 sts, sc next 2 sts tog, (sc in next 5 sts, sc next 2 sts tog) 2 times, sc in next 6 sts, changing to Green (cloth color) in last 2 loops of last st. (21)
Rnd 5: Sc in each st around.
Rnd 6: Working in back loops only. Sc in each st around.
Rnd 7: (Sc in next 5 sts, sc next 2 sts tog) around. (18)
Rnd 8: Sc in each st around.
Rnd 9: (Sc next 2 sts tog, sc in next st) around, changing to Cream in last 2 loops of last st. (12)
Rnd 10: (2 sc in next st, sc in next st) around. (18)
Rnd 11: (Sc in next 2 sts, 2 sc in next st) around. (24)
Rnd 12: Sc in next st, 2 sc in next st, (sc in next 3 sts, 2 sc in next st) 5 times, sc in next 2 sts. (30)
Rnd 13: (Sc in next 4 sts, 2 sc in next st) around. (36)
Rnd 14-16: Sc in each st around, changing to Brown (hair color) in last 2 loops of last st.
Rnd 17: Sc in each st around.
Rnd 18: Working in back loops only. (Sc next 2 sts tog, sc in next 4 sts) around. (30)
Rnd 19: Sc in next 2 sts, sc next 2 sts tog, (sc in next 3 sts, sc next 2 sts tog) 5 times, sc in next st. (24)
Rnd 20: (Sc next 2 sts tog, sc in next 2 sts) around. Stuff. (18)
Rnd 21: (Sc in next st, sc next 2 sts tog) around. (12)
Rnd 22: Sc next 2 sts tog around, sl st in first st. Fasten off. Sew opening close. (6)

Skirt

Rnd 1: Working in front loops of round 5 of the body and head pointed towards you. With Green, join with sl st , ch 1, 2 sc in same st, 2 sc in each st around. (42)
Rnd 2-6: Sc in each st around.
Rnd 7: Sc in each st around, sl st in first st. Fasten off.

Skirt for Red Girl:
Rnd 1-5: Same as above.
Rnd 6: Sc in each st around, changing to White in last 2 loops of last st.
Rnd 7: Sl st in next st, reverse sc in each st around, join with sl st in first st. Fasten off.

Reverse sc is working from left to right, insert hook in next st to the right and complete as sc.

Arm

Make 2.
Rnd 1: With Cream, ch 2, 6 sc in second chain from hook. (6)
Rnd 2-3: Sc in each st around.
Rnd 4: Sc in each st around, sl st in first st. Fasten off.

Arms for Pink Girl:
Rnd 1-2: Cream color.
Rnd 3-4: Pink color.
Do not stuff arms, sew arms to body.

Hair

With Brown. Cut 24 pieces of yarn, 6.5"(16.5 cm) long. For hair, hold one strand of yarn, fold in half. With top of the head facing, insert hook towards outer of head in free loops on rnd 17, draw the folded end through the stitch and pull the loose ends through the folded end, draw the knot up tightly. Add hair from one side of head to the back of head and from here to the other side of head. Do not add hair in the front (12 sts).

Flower

Ch 3, dc in first chain*, ch 2, sl st in first ch*, (ch 2, dc in first ch*, ch 2, sl st in first ch*) 4 times, fasten off.

* first chain = the first starting chain

Green & Yellow Girls

Green and Yellow Hats

Make one each: Green and Yellow.

Rnd 1: With Green, ch 2, 6 sc in second chain from hook. (6)
Rnd 2: 2 sc in each st around. (12)
Rnd 3: (Sc in next st, 2 sc in next st) around. (18)
Rnd 4: (2 sc in next st, sc in next 2 sts) around. (24)
Rnd 5: (Sc in next 3 sts, 2 sc in next st) around. (30)
Rnd 6: Sc in next st, 2sc in next st, (sc in next 4 sts, 2sc in next st) 5 times, sc in next 3 sts.(36)
Rnd 7-10: Sc in each st around.
Rnd 11: Sc in each st around, join with sl st in first st. Fasten off.

Green Hat

Make one Orange flower and one small Yellow flower.

Orange flower: same as flower pattern on page 21.

Small Yellow flower: Ch 4, sl st in first chain*, (ch 3, sl st in first ch*) 4 times, fasten off.

* first chain = the first starting chain

Sew Yellow flower on top of Orange flower with white bead in the middle. Sew it on the hat.

Yellow Hat

Make 5 Orange flowers and 5 Green flowers: Same as flower pattern on page 21.

Sew flowers on hat with white bead in the middle as in pictures.

Finishing

Put hat on head and sew it to head. Sew eyes 8 sts apart between rnds 14-15 of head. With Black embroidery floss, embroider eyelashes. With Red, embroider mouth on rnd 13.

Red & Purple Girls

Hat

Make one each: Red and Purple:

Rnd 1: With Red, ch 2, 6 sc in second chain from hook. (6)

Rnd 2: 2 sc in each st around. (12)

Rnd 3: (Sc in next st, 2 sc in next st) around. (18)

Rnd 4: (2 sc in next st, sc in next 2 sts) around. (24)

Rnd 5: (Sc in next 3 sts, 2 sc in next st) around. (30)

Rnd 6: Sc in next st, 2sc in next st, (sc in next 4 sts, 2sc in next st) 5 times, sc in next 3 sts.(36)

Rnd 7: Working in back loops only. Sc in each st around.

Rnd 8-11: Sc in each st around, changing to White in last 2 loops of last st.

Rnd 12: Sl st in next st, reverse sc in each st around, join with sl st in first st. Fasten off.

* You can do sc instead of reverse sc on round 12. *

For Purple Hat

Do not change color on rnd 11.

Rnd 12: Sc in each st around, join with sl st in first st. Fasten off.

Make one pink flower, same as flower pattern on page 21.

Sew it on hat with white bead in the middle.

Finishing

Put hat on head and sew it to head. Sew eyes 8 sts apart between rnds 13-14 of head. With Black embroidery floss, embroider eyelashes. With Red, embroider mouth on rnd 12.

Light Blue & Pink Girls

Hat

Make one each: Light Blue and Pink.

Rnd 1: With Light Blue, ch 2, 6 sc in second chain from hook. (6)

Rnd 2: 2 sc in each st around. (12)

Rnd 3: (Sc in next st, 2 sc in next st) around. (18)

Rnd 4: (2 sc in next st, sc in next 2 sts) around. (24)

Rnd 5: (Sc in next 3 sts, 2 sc in next st) around. (30)

Rnd 6: Sc in next st, 2sc in next st, (sc in next 4 sts, 2sc in next st) 5 times, sc in next 3 sts.(36)

Rnd 7-12: Sc in each st around.

Rnd 13: Working in front loops only. (2 sc in next st, sc in next 2 sts) around. (48)

Rnd 14: Sc in each st around.

Rnd 15: (2 sc in next st, sc in next 3 sts) around. (60)

Rnd 16: Sc in each st around, join with sl st in first st. Fasten off.

Cut yarn 15" (38 cm) long, one each in blue, pink and white yarn. Insert hook through one stitch on round 12, pull out the yarns, put yarns around the hat, insert hook through one stitch on round 12, pull out the yarns, tie bow.

Finishing

Put hat on head and sew it to head. Sew eyes 8 sts apart between rnds 13-14 of head. With Black embroidery floss, embroider eyelashes. With Red, embroider mouth on rnd 12.

Puffy Pals

Material

- Sport, Baby  Catania yarn from Schachenmayr SMC. (White, Black, Green, Brown, Pink, Dark Pink, Red, Peach and Yellow).
- 3.00 mm hook.
- Black and white embroidery floss.
- Polyester fiberfill.
- 6 pairs of 6mm safety eyes.
- 3 white 7mm buttons for cat eyes and pig snout.
- 2 black 5mm beads for frog eyes.
- Tapestry needle.
- Sewing needle and thread for attaching cat eyes.
- Pins

Size: The dolls are 2.4 inches or 6 cm high (this excludes the ears).

Remarks

- This project is working in continuous rounds, do not join or turn unless otherwise stated. Mark first stitch of each round.
- The animals have the same basic pattern for body and feet.

Body

Make one for each animal.

Rnd 1: With body color (Brown for the bear), ch 11, sc in second chain from hook, sc in next 8 chs, 3 sc in last ch; working in remaining loops on opposite side of chain, sc in next 8 chs, 2 sc in next ch. (22)

	x	x	x	x	x	x	x	x	x	x	o
x	o	o	o	o	o	o	o	o	o	o	x
	x	x	x	x	x	x	x	x	x	x	

o = chain   x = sc

Rnd 2: 2 sc in next st, sc in next 8 sts, 2 sc in next 3 sts, sc in next 8 sts, 2 sc in next 2 sts. (28)
Rnd 3: 2 sc in next st, sc in next 10 sts, 2 sc in next st, sc in next 2 sts, 2 sc in next st, sc in next 10 sts, 2 sc in next st, sc in next 2 sts. (32)
Rnd 4: 2 sc in next st, sc in next 12 sts, 2 sc in next st, sc in next 2 sts, 2 sc in next st, sc in next 12 sts, 2 sc in next st, sc in next 2 sts. (36)
Rnd 5-9: Sc in each st around. (36)
Rnd 10: (Sc in next 16 sts, sc next 2 sts tog) 2 times. (34)
Rnd 11: (Sc in next 15 sts, sc next 2 sts tog) 2 times. (32)
Rnd 12: Sc in next 7 sts, sc next 2 sts tog, sc in next 14 sts, sc next 2 sts tog, sc in next 7 sts. (30)
Rnd 13: (Sc in next 13 sts, sc next 2 sts tog) 2 times. (28)
Rnd 14: Sc in next 6 sts, sc next 2 sts tog, sc in next 12 sts, sc next 2 sts tog, sc in next 6 sts. (26)
Rnd 15: (Sc in next 11 sts, sc next 2 sts tog) 2 times. (24)
Rnd 16: (Sc in next 2 sts, sc next 2 sts tog) around. (18)

Put safety eyes 3-4 sts apart, between rnd 13-14 of body. Stuff.

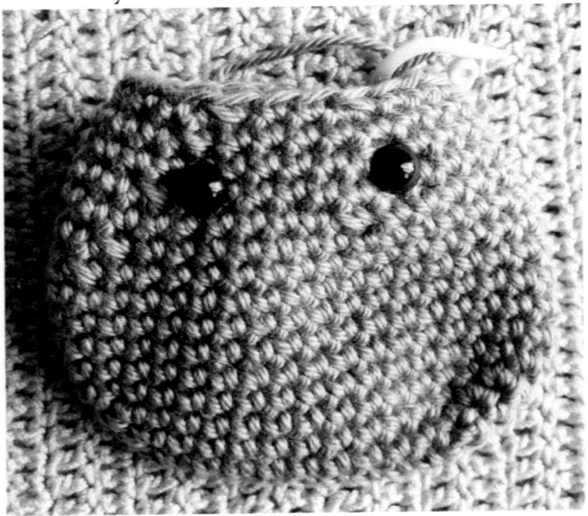

Rnd 17: (Sc in next st, sc next 2 sts tog) around. (12)
Rnd 18: Sc next 2 sts tog around, join with sl st in first st, fasten off. (6)

For hair on top of the Ducky only: after finished Rnd 18 do not fasten off.

Duckies' Hair: ch 4, sl st in second chain from hook, sl st in next 2 chs, sc in next st, ch 6, sl st in second chain from hook, sl st in next 4 chs, sc in next st, ch 3, sl st in second chain from hook, sl st in next ch, sl st in next st, Fasten off (see diagram on page 15). Sew opening close.

Feet

Make two for each animal.

Rnd 1: With feet color (Brown for the bear), ch 7, sc in second chain from hook, sc in next 4 chs, 3 sc in last ch; working in remaining loops on opposite side of chain, sc in next 4 chs, 2 sc in next ch. (14)

	x	x	x	x	x	x	o
x	o	o	o	o	o	o	x
	x	x	x	x	x	x	

o = chain x = sc

Rnd 2: 2 sc in next st, sc in next 4 sts, 2 sc in next 3 sts, sc in next 4 sts, 2 sc in next 2 sts. (20)

Rnd 3-4: Sc in each st around. (20)

Rnd 5: (Sc next 2 sts tog, sc in next 6 sts, sc next 2 sts tog) 2 times. (16)

Rnd 6: (Sc next 2 sts tog, sc in next 4 sts, sc next 2 sts tog) 2 times, join with sl st in first st. Leave long end for sewing, fasten off. (12)

Stuff and pin feet on bottom of the body and sew.

Rabbit

Rabbit Ear

Make 2.

Rnd 1: With Red, ch 2, 6 sc in second chain from hook. (6)

Rnd 2: (Sc in next st, 2 sc in next st) around. (9)

Rnd 3: (Sc in next 2 sts, 2 sc in next st) around. (12)

Rnd 4: (Sc in next 3 sts, 2 sc in next st) around, changing to Dark Pink in last two loops of last st. (15)

Rnd 5-7: Sc in each st around. (15)

Rnd 8: (Sc next 2 sts tog, sc in next 3 sts) around, changing to Pink in last two loops of last st. (12)

Rnd 9: (Sc next 2 sts tog, sc in next 2 sts) around. (9)

Rnd 10: (Sc next 2 sts tog, sc in next st) around. (6)

Rnd 11: Sc in each st around, join with sl st in first st. Leave long end for sewing, fasten off.

Finishing

Sew ears on the middle top of the body. With Black embroidery floss, embroider mouth.

Frog

Frog Eye

Make 2.

Rnd 1: With Green, ch 2, 6 sc in second chain from hook. (6)

Rnd 2: (Sc in next st, 2 sc in next st) around. (9)

Rnd 3: Sc in each st around. (9)

Rnd 4: Sc in each st around, join with sl st in first st. Leave long end for sewing, fasten off. (9)

Sew beads in middle of eyes.

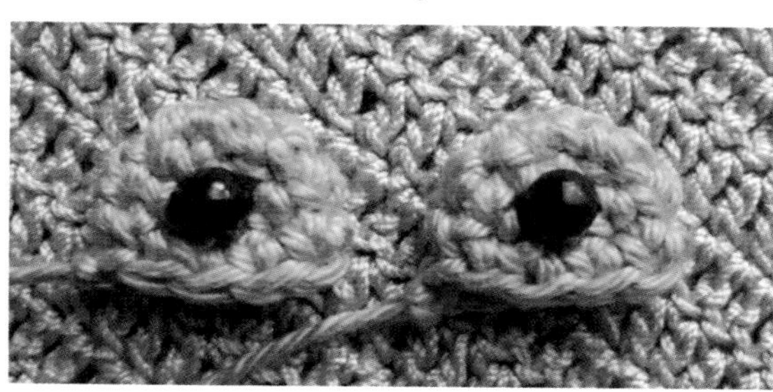

Finishing

Sew eyes on rnds 15-18 of body.
With Black embroidery floss, embroider mouth on rnd 14.

Bear

Bear Ear

Make 2.

Rnd 1: With Brown, ch 2, 6 sc in second chain from hook. (6)

Rnd 2: (Sc in next st, 2 sc in next st) around. (9)

Rnd 3: Sc in each st around. (9)

Rnd 4: Sc in each st around, join with sl st in first st. Leave long end for sewing, fasten off. (9)

Finishing

Pin ears on rnds 11-15 and sew.

With Black embroidery floss, embroider nose.

Piglet

Pig Ear

Make 2.

Rnd 1: With Peach, ch 2, 4 sc in second chain from hook. (4)

Rnd 2: (Sc in next st, 2 sc in next st) 2 times. (6)

Rnd 3: (Sc in next st, 2 sc in next st) around. (9)

Rnd 4: (Sc in next 2 sts, 2 sc in next st) around, join with sl st in first st. Leave long end for sewing, fasten off. (12)

Finishing

Pin ears on rnds 14-18 and sew.

Pig Snout: Sew a white button on rnds 12-13 as in picture.

Ducky

Duck Beak

Working in rows.

Row 1: With Red, ch 4, 2 dc in the 4th chain from hook, turn. (count 3 chs as one dc, 3)

Row 2: Ch 3, dc next 2 sts tog, fasten off. (1)

Finishing

Fold mouth in half, pin it on rnd 12 and sew.

Cat

Cat Ear

Make 2.

Rnd 1: With Black, ch 2, 4 sc in second chain from hook. (4)

Rnd 2: (Sc in next st, 2 sc in next st) 2 times. (6)

Rnd 3: (Sc in next st, 2 sc in next st) around. (9)

Rnd 4: (Sc in next 2 sts, 2 sc in next st) around, join with sl st in first st. Leave long end for sewing, fasten off. (12)

Finishing

Pin ears on rnds 13-17 and sew. Sew white buttons (eyes) 3 sts apart on rnds 13-15 as in picture above.

With White embroidery floss, embroider nose as in picture.

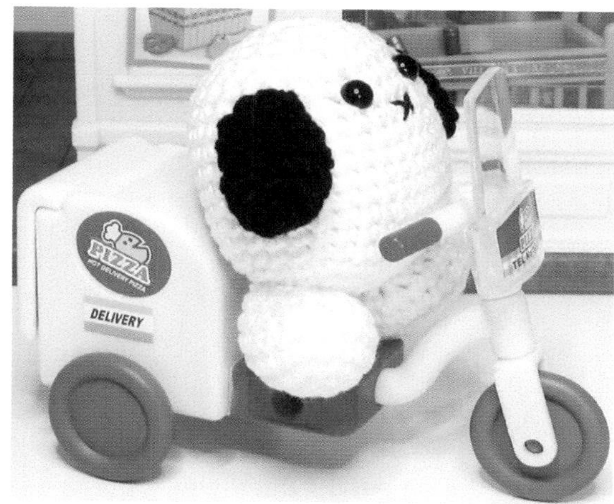

Puppy

Puppy Ear

Make 2.

Rnd 1: With Black, ch 2, 6 sc in second chain from hook. (6)
Rnd 2: 2 sc in each st around. (12)
Rnd 3-4: Sc in each st around. (12)
Rnd 5: (Sc next 2 sts tog, sc in next 2 sts) around. (9)
Rnd 6-7: Sc in each st around. (9)
Rnd 8: (Sc next 2 sts tog, sc in next st) around, join with sl st in first st. Leave long end for sewing, fasten off. (6)

Finishing

Pin ears on rnd 13 and sew.
With Black embroidery floss, embroider nose as in picture below.

Garden Pals

Material

- Sport, Baby Catania yarn from Schachenmayr SMC; White, Light Yellow, Yellow, Green, Light Green, Black, Brown, Pink, Peach, Red and Blue (yarn used for one doll - 10-15g).
- 3.25 mm hook (US: D/3.25, UK: 10).
- 7 pairs of 6 mm safety eyes.
- 2 black 5 mm beads for owl eyes.
- Polyester fiberfill = 80 g (10 g/ doll).
- Tapestry needle.
- Sewing needle and thread for attaching owl eyes.
- Pins.

Size: The dolls are 3 inches or 7.5 cm high (this excludes the ears).

Remarks

- All Garden Pals have the same Feet Pattern as Puffy Pals. See the Feet pattern on page 27.
- The Bee, Butterfly, Ladybird, Caterpillar and Owl have the same Body pattern as Puffy Pals. See the Body pattern on page 26.
- This project is working in continuous rounds, do not join or turn unless otherwise stated. Mark first stitch of each round.

Buzzy Bee

Body

Follow the instructions for the Body pattern on page 26 and change colors as stated below.

Rnd 1-4: Yellow color
Rnd 5-6: Brown color
Rnd 7-9: Yellow color
Rnd 10-11: Brown color
Rnd 12-18: Yellow color

Feet

Follow the Feet pattern on page 27. Make 2 in Brown color.

Antenna

Make 2 in brown color.

Rnd 1: Ch 6, 4 sc in second chain from hook, sl st in next 4 chs, leave long end for sewing, fasten off. (8)

Wing

Make 2

Rnd 1: With White, ch 2, 6 sc in second chain from hook. (6)

Rnd 2: 2 sc in each st around. (12)

Rnd 3: (2 sc in next st, sc in next st) around. (18)

Rnd 4: (Sc in next 2 sts, 2 sc in next st) around, join with sl st in first st. Leave long end for sewing, fasten off. (24)

Finishing

Sew the last round of the 2 wings together for about 3-4 sts.

Sew wings on middle back of body.

Pin antenna on rnd 18 of body and sew.

Betty Butterfly

Body

Follow the instructions for the Body pattern on page 26 and change colors as stated below.

Rnd 1-11: Light Green color

Rnd 12-18: Peach color

Feet

Follow the Feet pattern on page 27, make 2 in Light Green color.

Wing

Make 2.

Rnd 1: With Light Green, ch 2, 6 sc in second chain from hook. (6)

Rnd 2: 2 sc in each st around, changing to Peach in last two loops of last st. (12)

Rnd 3: (2 sc in next st, sc in next st) around. (18)

Rnd 4: (Sc in next 2 sts, 2 sc in next st) around, changing to Light Yellow in last two loops of last st. (24)

Rnd 5: (2 sc in next st, sc in next 3 sts) around. (30)

Rnd 6: Sc in next 2 sts, 2 sc in next st, (sc in next 4 sts, 2 sc in next st) 5 times, sc in next 2 sts, join with sl st in first st. Leave long end for sewing, fasten off. (36)

Antenna

Make 2.

Rnd 1: Ch 6, 4 sc in second chain from hook, sl st in next 4 chs, leave long end for sewing, fasten off. (8)

Finishing

Sew last round of the 2 wings together for about 4-5 sts.

Sew wings on middle back of body.

Sew antenna on rnd 18 of body.

Leila Ladybird

Body

Follow the instructions of the Body pattern on page 26.

Rnd 1-18: Black color

Feet

Follow the Feet pattern on page 27, make 2 in Black color.

Antenna

Make 2 in Black color.

Rnd 1: Ch 6, 4 sc in second chain from hook, sl st in next 4 chs, leave long end for sewing, fasten off. (8)

Wing

Make 2

Rnd 1: With Red, ch 2, 6 sc in second chain from hook. (6)

Rnd 2: 2 sc in each st around. (12)

Rnd 3: (2 sc in next st, sc in next st) around. (18)

Rnd 4: (Sc in next 2 sts, 2 sc in next st) around. (24)

Rnd 5: (2 sc in next st, sc in next 3 sts) around. (30)

Rnd 6: Sc in next 2 sts, 2 sc in next st, (sc in next 4 sts, 2 sc in next st) 5 times, sc in next 2 sts. (36)

Fold wing in half, matching sts, working in rnd 6 through both thicknesses, sc in next 17 sts. Leave long end for sewing, fasten off.

With Black, embroider dots on wings as in picture below.

Finishing

Sew wings together as in picture. Sew wings on middle back of body. Sew antenna on rnd 18 of body.

Owlbert Owl

Body
Follow the instructions of the Body pattern on page 26.
Rnd 1-11: Blue color
Rnd 12-18: Pink color

Feet
Follow the Feet pattern on page 27, make 2 in Blue color.

Beak
Rnd 1: With Yellow, ch 2, 4 sc in second chain from hook. (4)
Rnd 2: (2 sc in next st, sc in next st) 2 times, join with sl st in first st. Leave long end for sewing, fasten off. (6)

Ear
Make 2.
Rnd 1: With Pink, ch 2, 4 sc in second chain from hook. (4)
Rnd 2: (2 sc in next st, sc in next st) 2 times. (6)
Rnd 3: (2 sc in next st, sc in next 2 sts) 2 times, join with sl st in first st. Leave long end for sewing, fasten off. (8)

Eye

Make 2.

Rnd 1: With White, ch 2, 6 sc in second chain from hook. (6)

Rnd 2: 2 sc in each st around, join with sl st in first st. Leave long end for sewing, fasten off. (12)

Sew beads on the middle of the eyes.

Finishing

Pin ears on rnds 15-17 and sew.

Pin beak on rnd 12 and sew.

Pin eyes on rnds 12-16 and sew.

Katie Caterpillar

Body

Follow the instructions of the Body pattern on page 26.
Rnd 1-3: Green color
Rnd 4-6: Light Green color
Rnd 7-9: Green color
Rnd 10-12: Light Green color
Rnd 13-18: Green color

Feet

Follow the Feet pattern on page 27, make 2 in Green color.

Antenna

Make 2 in light Green color.
Rnd 1: Ch 6, 4 sc in second chain from hook, sl st in next 4 chs, leave long end for sewing, fasten off. (8)

Finishing

Sew antenna on rnd 18 of body.

Daffy Daffodil

Body

Rnd 1: With Yellow, ch 11, sc in second chain from hook, sc in next 8 chs, 3 sc in last ch; working in remaining loops on opposite side of chain, sc in next 8 chs, 2 sc in next ch. (22)

x x x x x x x x x x o

x o o o o o o o o o o x

x x x x x x x x x x

o = chain x = sc

Rnd 2: 2 sc in next st, sc in next 8 sts, 2 sc in next 3 sts, sc in next 8 sts, 2 sc in next 2 sts. (28)

Rnd 3: 2 sc in next st, sc in next 10 sts, 2 sc in next st, sc in next 2 sts, 2 sc in next st, sc in next 10 sts, 2 sc in next st, sc in next 2 sts. (32)

Rnd 4: 2 sc in next st, sc in next 12 sts, 2 sc in next st, sc in next 2 sts, 2 sc in next st, sc in next 12 sts, 2 sc in next st, sc in next 2 sts. (36)

Rnd 5: Working in back loops only. Sc in each st around. (36)

Rnd 6-7: Sc in each st around. (36)

Rnd 8: Sc in each st around, changing to Light Yellow in last two loops of last st. (36)

Rnd 9: Sc in each st around. (36)

Rnd 10: Working in back loops only. (Sc in next 16 sts, sc next 2 sts tog) 2 times. (34)

Rnd 11: (Sc in next 15 sts, sc next 2 sts tog) 2 times. (32)

Rnd 12: Sc in next 7 sts, sc next 2 sts tog, sc in next 14 sts, sc next 2 sts tog, sc in next 7 sts. (30)

Rnd 13: (Sc in next 13 sts, sc next 2 sts tog) 2 times. (28)
Rnd 14: Sc in next 6 sts, sc next 2 sts tog, sc in next 12 sts, sc next 2 sts tog, sc in next 6 sts. (26)
Rnd 15: (Sc in next 11 sts, sc next 2 sts tog) 2 times. (24)
Rnd 16: (Sc in next 2 sts, sc next 2 sts tog) around. (18)

Put safety eyes 3-4 sts apart, between rnd 13-14 of body. Stuff.

Rnd 17: (Sc in next st, sc next 2 sts tog) around. (12)
Rnd 18: Sc next 2 sts tog around, join with sl st in first st, fasten off.

Edge of Cup

Working in free loops of rnd 4, with Yellow, join yarn to free loop of rnd 4, sc in same st, (ch 3, sc in next st) around, fasten off.

Petals

Working in rows.

First Petal

Row 1: Working in free loops of rnd 9, with Light Yellow, join yarn to free loop of rnd 9, ch 1, sc in same st, sc in next 5 sts, turn. (6)

Row 2-3: Ch 1, sc in each st across, turn. (6)
Row 4: Ch 1, sc first 2 sts tog, sc in next 2 sts, sc next 2 sts tog, turn. (4)
Row 5: Ch 1, sc first 2 sts tog, sc next 2 sts tog, turn. (2)
Row 6: Ch 1, sc first 2 sts tog, turn. (1)
Row 7: Ch 1; working in ends of rows, sl st in next 6 rows (end of rows 6-1), sl st in next free loop of rnd 9.

<u>Second – Sixth Petals</u>
Row 1: Ch 1, sc in same st, sc in next 5 sts, turn. (6)

Row 2-3: Ch 1, sc in each st across, turn. (6)
Row 4: Ch 1, sc first 2 sts tog, sc in next 2 sts, sc next 2 sts tog, turn. (4)
Row 5: Ch 1, sc first 2 sts tog, sc next 2 sts tog, turn. (2)
Row 6: Ch 1, sc first 2 sts tog, turn. (1)
Row 7: Ch 1; working in ends of rows, sl st in next 6 rows (end of rows 6-1), sl st in next free loop of rnd 9.

Feet

Follow the Feet pattern on page 27, make 2 feet in Yellow color.

Daffodil Stem

Rnd 1: With Green, ch 2, 6 sc in second chain from hook. (6)
Rnd 2-5: Sc in each st around. (6)
Rnd 6: 2 sc in each st around, join with sl st in first st. Leave long end for sewing, fasten off. (12)

Finishing

Sew stem on middle top.

Dancy Daisy

Body

Rnd 1: With Green, ch 11, sc in second chain from hook, sc in next 8 chs, 3 sc in last ch; working in remaining loops on opposite side of chain, sc in next 8 chs, 2 sc in next ch. (22)

```
    x  x  x  x  x  x  x  x  x  x  o
 x  o  o  o  o  o  o  o  o  o  o  x
    x  x  x  x  x  x  x  x  x  x
```

o = chain   x = sc

Rnd 2: 2 sc in next st, sc in next 8 sts, 2 sc in next 3 sts, sc in next 8 sts, 2 sc in next 2 sts. (28)
Rnd 3: 2 sc in next st, sc in next 10 sts, 2 sc in next st, sc in next 2 sts, 2 sc in next st, sc in next 10 sts, 2 sc in next st, sc in next 2 sts. (32)
Rnd 4: 2 sc in next st, sc in next 12 sts, 2 sc in next st, sc in next 2 sts, 2 sc in next st, sc in next 12 sts, 2 sc in next st, sc in next 2 sts. (36)
Rnd 5-9: Sc in each st around. (36)
Rnd 10: (Sc in next 16 sts, sc next 2 sts tog) 2 times. (34)
Rnd 11: (Sc in next 15 sts, sc next 2 sts tog) 2 times, changing to Yellow in last two loops of last st. (32)
Rnd 12: Working in back loops only. Sc in next 7 sts, sc next 2 sts tog, sc in next 14 sts, sc next 2 sts tog, sc in next 7 sts. (30)
Rnd 13: (Sc in next 13 sts, sc next 2 sts tog) 2 times. (28)
Rnd 14: Sc in next 6 sts, sc next 2 sts tog, sc in next 12 sts, sc next 2 sts tog, sc in next 6 sts. (26)

Rnd 15: (Sc in next 11 sts, sc next 2 sts tog) 2 times. (24)
Rnd 16: (Sc in next 2 sts, sc next 2 sts tog) around. (18)

Put safety eyes 3-4 sts apart, between rnd 13-14 of body. Stuff.

Rnd 17: (Sc in next st, sc next 2 sts tog) around. (12)
Rnd 18: Sc next 2 sts tog around, join with sl st in first st, fasten off.

Feet

Follow the Feet pattern on page 27, make 2 feet in Green color.

Petals

Rnd 1: Working in free loops of rnd 11, with White, join yarn to free loop of rnd 11, ch 1, sc in each st around. (32)
Rnd 2: Sl st in next st, (ch 5, sc in second chain from hook, sc in next 3 chs, sl st in next st on rnd 1) around, fasten off.

Finished

Tulipa Tulip

Body

Rnd 1: With Pink, ch 11, sc in second chain from hook, sc in next 8 chs, 3 sc in last ch; working in remaining loops on opposite side of chain, sc in next 8 chs, 2 sc in next ch. (22)

```
  x x x x x x x x x x o
x o o o o o o o o o o x
  x x x x x x x x x x
```

o = chain x = sc

Rnd 2: 2 sc in next st, sc in next 8 sts, 2 sc in next 3 sts, sc in next 8 sts, 2 sc in next 2 sts. (28)

Rnd 3: 2 sc in next st, sc in next 10 sts, 2 sc in next st, sc in next 2 sts, 2 sc in next st, sc in next 10 sts, 2 sc in next st, sc in next 2 sts. (32)

Rnd 4: 2 sc in next st, sc in next 12 sts, 2 sc in next st, sc in next 2 sts, 2 sc in next st, sc in next 12 sts, 2 sc in next st, sc in next 2 sts. (36)

Rnd 5-6: Sc in each st around. (36)

Rnd 7: Working in back loops only. Sc in each st around. (36)

Rnd 8-9: Sc in each st around. (36)

Rnd 10: (Sc in next 16 sts, sc next 2 sts tog) 2 times. (34)

Rnd 11: (Sc in next 15 sts, sc next 2 sts tog) 2 times. (32)

Rnd 12: Sc in next 7 sts, sc next 2 sts tog, sc in next 14 sts, sc next 2 sts tog, sc in next 7 sts. (30)

Rnd 13: (Sc in next 13 sts, sc next 2 sts tog) 2 times. (28)

Rnd 14: Sc in next 6 sts, sc next 2 sts tog, sc in next 12 sts, sc next 2 sts tog, sc in next 6 sts. (26)

Rnd 15: (Sc in next 11 sts, sc next 2 sts tog) 2 times. (24)
Rnd 16: (Sc in next 2 sts, sc next 2 sts tog) around. (18)

Put safety eyes 3-4 sts apart, between rnd 13-14 of body. Stuff.

Rnd 17: (Sc in next st, sc next 2 sts tog) around. (12)
Rnd 18: Sc next 2 sts tog around, join with sl st in first st, fasten off.

Petals

Working in rows.

__First Petal__

Row 1: Working in free loops of rnd 6, with pink, join yarn to free loop of rnd 6, ch 1, sc in same st, sc in next 5 sts, turn. (6)

Row 2-3: Ch 1, sc in each st across, turn. (6)
Row 4: Ch 1, sc first 3 sts tog, sc in next 3 sts tog, turn. (2)
Row 5: Ch 1, sc first 2 sts tog; working in ends of rows, sl st in next 4 rows (end of rows 5-1), sl st in next free loop of rnd 6.

__Second – Sixth Petals__

Row 1: Ch 1, sc in same st, sc in next 5 sts, turn. (6)
Row 2-3: Ch 1, sc in each st across, turn. (6)
Row 4: Ch 1, sc first 3 sts tog, sc in next 3 sts tog, turn. (2)
Row 5: Ch 1, sc first 2 sts tog; working in ends of rows, sl st in next 4 rows (end of rows 5-1), sl st in next free loop of rnd 6.

Stem

Rnd 1: With Green, ch 2, 6 sc in second chain from hook. (6)
Rnd 2-5: Sc in each st around. (6)
Rnd 6: 2 sc in each st around. (12)
Rnd 7: (Sl st in next st, ch 3, sl st in next st) around. Leave long end for sewing, fasten off.

Feet

Follow the Feet pattern on page 27, make 2 feet in Pink color.

Finishing

Sew stem on middle top.

Pillow Pals

Remarks

- This project is working in continuous rounds, do not join or turn unless otherwise stated. Mark first stitch of each round.
- All Animals have the same basic pattern for Body and Feet.

Size

Pillow Pals are 14 inches/ 35 cm high (excluding ears).

Body Pattern

Rnd 1: Ch 31, sc in second chain from hook, sc in next 28 chs, 3 sc in last ch; working in remaining loops on opposite side of chain, sc in next 28 chs, 2 sc in next ch. (62)

```
  x  x  x  x  ...  ...  ...  x  x  x  o
x  o  o  o  o  ...  ...  ...  o  o  o  x
  x  x  x  x  ...  ...  ...  x  x  x
```

o = chain x = sc

Rnd 2: 2 sc in next st, sc in next 28 sts, 2 sc in next 3 sts, sc in next 28 sts, 2 sc in next 2 sts. (68)

Rnd 3: 2 sc in next st, sc in next 30 sts, 2 sc in next st, sc in next 2 sts, 2 sc in next st, sc in next 30 sts, 2 sc in next st, sc in next 2 sts. (72)
Rnd 4: 2 sc in next st, sc in next 32 sts, 2 sc in next st, sc in next 2 sts, 2 sc in next st, sc in next 32 sts, 2 sc in next st, sc in next 2 sts. (76)
Rnd 5: 2 sc in next st, sc in next 34 sts, 2 sc in next st, sc in next 2 sts, 2 sc in next st, sc in next 34 sts, 2 sc in next st, sc in next 2 sts. (80)
Rnd 6: 2 sc in next st, sc in next 36 sts, 2 sc in next st, sc in next 2 sts, 2 sc in next st, sc in next 36 sts, 2 sc in next st, sc in next 2 sts. (84)
Rnd 7: 2 sc in next st, sc in next 38 sts, 2 sc in next st, sc in next 2 sts, 2 sc in next st, sc in next 38 sts, 2 sc in next st, sc in next 2 sts. (88)
Rnd 8-22: Sc in each st around. (88)
Rnd 23: (Sc in next 42 sts, sc next 2 sts tog) 2 times. (86)
Rnd 24: (Sc next 2 sts tog, sc in next 41 sts) 2 times. (84)
Rnd 25: Sc in each st around. (84)
Rnd 26: (Sc in next 40 sts, sc next 2 sts tog) 2 times. (82)
Rnd 27: (Sc next 2 sts tog, sc in next 39 sts) 2 times. (80)
Rnd 28: Sc in each st around. (80)
Rnd 29: (Sc in next 38 sts, sc next 2 sts tog) 2 times. (78)
Rnd 30: (Sc next 2 sts tog, sc in next 37 sts) 2 times. (76)
Rnd 31: (Sc in next 17 sts, sc next 2 sts tog) around. (72)
Rnd 32: Sc in next 5 sts, sc next 2 sts tog, (sc in next 10 sts, sc next 2 sts tog) 5 times, sc in next 5 sts. (66)
Rnd 33: (Sc in next 9 sts, sc next 2 sts tog) around. (60)
Rnd 34: Sc in next 4 sts, sc next 2 sts tog, (sc in next 8 sts, sc next 2 sts tog) 5 times, sc in next 4 sts. (54)
Rnd 35: (Sc in next 7 sts, sc next 2 sts tog) around. (48)
Rnd 36: Sc in next 3 sts, sc next 2 sts tog, (sc in next 6 sts, sc next 2 sts tog) 5 times, sc in next 3 sts. (42)
Rnd 37: (Sc in next 5 sts, sc next 2 sts tog) around. (36)
Rnd 38: Sc in next 2 sts, sc next 2 sts tog, (sc in next 4 sts, sc next 2 sts tog) 5 times, sc in next 2 sts. (30)

Put safety eyes 10 sts apart, between rnd 25-26 of body. Stuff.

Rnd 39: (Sc in next 3 sts, sc next 2 sts tog) around. (24)
Rnd 40: (Sc in next 2 sts, sc next 2 sts tog) around. (18)
Rnd 41: (Sc in next st, sc next 2 sts tog) around. Stuff more tightly. (12)
Rnd 42: Sc next 2 sts tog around, join with sl st to first st, fasten off. (6)

Feet Pattern

Make 2.

Rnd 1: Ch 15, sc in second chain from hook, sc in next 12 chs, 3 sc in last ch; working in remaining loops on opposite side of chain, sc in next 12 chs, 2 sc in next ch. (30)

```
  x x x x … … … x x x o
x o o o o … … … o o o x
  x x x x … … … x x x
```

o = chain x = sc

Rnd 2: 2 sc in next st, sc in next 12 sts, 2 sc in next 3 sts, sc in next 12 sts, 2 sc in next 2 sts. (36)
Rnd 3: Sc in next st, 2 sc in next st, sc in next 13 sts, 2 sc in next st, (sc in next st, 2 sc in next st) 2 times, sc in next 13 sts, 2 sc in next st, sc in next st, 2 sc in next st. (42)
Rnd 4: 2 sc in next st, sc in next 14 sts, 2 sc in next st, (sc in next 2 sts, 2 sc in next st) 2 times, sc in next 14 sts, (2 sc in next st, sc in next 2 sts) 2 times. (48)
Rnd 5: Sc in next 3 sts, 2 sc in next st, sc in next 15 sts, 2 sc in next st, (sc in next 3 sts, 2 sc in next st) 2 times, sc in next 15 sts, 2 sc in next st, sc in next 3 sts, 2 sc in next st. (54)
Rnd 6: 2 sc in next st, sc in next 16 sts, 2 sc in next st, (sc in next 4 sts, 2 sc in next st) 2 times, sc in next 16 sts, (2 sc in next st, sc in next 4 sts) 2 times. (60)
Rnd 7-11: Sc in each st around. (60)
Rnd 12: Sc in next 4 sts, sc next 2 sts tog, (sc in next 8 sts, sc next 2 sts tog) 5 times, sc in next 4 sts. (54)
Rnd 13: (Sc in next 7 sts, sc next 2 sts tog) around. (48)
Rnd 14: Sc in next 3 sts, sc next 2 sts tog, (sc in next 6 sts, sc next 2 sts tog) 5 times, sc in next 3 sts. (42)
Rnd 15: (Sc next 2 sts tog) 3 times, sc in next 9 sts, (sc next 2 sts tog) 6 times, sc in next 9 sts, (sc next 2 sts tog) 3 times. (30)
Rnd 16: (Sc next 2 sts tog) 2 times, sc in next 7 sts, (sc next 2 sts tog) 4 times, sc in next 7 sts, (sc next 2 sts tog) 2 times. (22)
Rnd 17: Sc in each st around, join with sl st in first st, leave long end for sewing, fasten off. (22) Stuff feet.

Sew feet on bottom of the body.

Piggy

Material

- Chunky, Craft, Rug **5 Bulky**
  Sirdar Hayfield Bonus Chunky yarns:
  Bubblegum (776) = 250 g and Black (965) = 5 g
- 6.00 mm hook.
- Polyester fibrefill 600 g
- 15 mm safety eyes
- Tapestry needle.
- Pins

For body only (without feet) use:

- Sirdar Hayfield Bonus Chunky yarns:
  Bubblegum (776) = 190 g and Black (965) = 5 g
- Polyester fibrefill 450 g

Body

With color pink (bubblegum 776), follow the instructions of Body Pattern on page 52.

Feet

Make 2 feet in Pink (Bubblegum 776) color, follow the Feet Pattern on page 53.

Ear

Make 2 in Pink (Bubblegum 776) color.

Rnd 1: Ch 2, 6 sc in second chain from hook. (6)
Rnd 2: (Sc in next st, 2 sc in next st) around. (9)
Rnd 3: (2 sc in next st, sc in next 2 sts) around. (12)
Rnd 4: (Sc in next 3 sts, 2 sc in next st) around. (15)
Rnd 5: Sc in next 2 sts, 2 sc in next st, (sc in next 4 sts, 2 sc in next st) 2 times, sc in next 2 sts. (18)
Rnd 6: (Sc in next 5 sts, 2 sc in next st) around. (21)
Rnd 7: Sc in next 3 sts, 2 sc in next st, (sc in next 6 sts, 2 sc in next st) 2 times, sc in next 3 sts. (24)
Rnd 8: Sc in each st around. (24)
Rnd 9: (Sc next 2 sts tog, sc in next 2 sts) around, join with sl st in first st. Leave long end for sewing, fasten off. (18)

Sew the opening close flat.

Pig Snout

Rnd 1: With Pink (Bubblegum 776), ch 2, 6 sc in second chain from hook. (6)
Rnd 2: 2 sc in each st around. (12)
Rnd 3: (Sc in next st, 2 sc in next st) around. (18)
Rnd 4: (2 sc in next st, sc in next 2 sts) around. (24)
Rnd 5: Working in back loops only. Sc in each st around. (24)
Rnd 6: Sc in each st around, join with sl st in first st, leave long end for sewing, fasten off. (24)
With Black yarn, embroider 2 lines as in picture.

Finishing

Pin ears on rnds 25-34 and sew. Sew pig snout on rnds 20-27 and stuff before sewing the opening close.

Doggy

Material

- Chunky, Craft, Rug Sirdar Hayfield Bonus Chunky yarns: Black (965) = 55 g and White (961) = 210 g
- 6.00 mm hook.
- Polyester fibrefill 600 g
- 15 mm safety eyes
- Tapestry needle.
- Pins

For body only (without feet) use:

- Sirdar Hayfield Bonus Chunky yarns: Black (965) = 55 g and White (776) = 150 g
- Polyester fibrefill 450 g

Body

With color White (961), follow the instructions of Body Pattern on page 52.

Feet

Make 2 feet in White (961) color, follow the Feet Pattern on page 53.

Ear

Make 2 in Black (965) color.

Rnd 1: Ch 11, sc in second chain from hook, sc in next 8 chs, 3 sc in last ch; working in remaining loops on opposite side of chain, sc in next 8 chs, 2 sc in next ch. (22)

```
  x x x x x x x x x x o
x o o o o o o o o o o x
  x x x x x x x x x x
```

o = chain   x = sc

Rnd 2: 2 sc in next st, sc in next 8 sts, 2 sc in next 3 sts, sc in next 8 sts, 2 sc in next 2 sts. (28)
Rnd 3: 2 sc in next st, sc in next 10 sts, 2 sc in next st, sc in next 2 sts, 2 sc in next st, sc in next 10 sts, 2 sc in next st, sc in next 2 sts. (32)
Rnd 4: 2 sc in next st, sc in next 12 sts, 2 sc in next st, sc in next 2 sts, 2 sc in next st, sc in next 12 sts, 2 sc in next st, sc in next 2 sts. (36)
Rnd 5-9: Sc in each st around. (36)
Rnd 10: (Sc in next 10 sts, sc next 2 sts tog) 3 times. (33)
Rnd 11: (Sc in next 9 sts, sc next 2 sts tog) 3 times. (30)
Rnd 12: Sc in each st around. (30)
Rnd 13: (Sc in next 8 sts, sc next 2 sts tog) 3 times. (27)
Rnd 14: Sc in each st around. (27)
Rnd 15: (Sc in next 7 sts, sc next 2 sts tog) 3 times. (24)
Rnd 16: Sc in each st around. (24)
Rnd 17: (Sc in next 6 sts, sc next 2 sts tog) 3 times. (21)
Rnd 18: Sc in each st around. (21)
Rnd 19: (Sc in next 5 sts, sc next 2 sts tog) 3 times. (18)
Rnd 20: Sc in each st around, join with sl st in first st, leave long end for sewing, fasten off. (18)
Sew the opening close flat.

Finishing

Pin ears on rnds 30 and sew. With Black yarn embroider nose as in picture (page 57).

Bear

Material

- Chunky, Craft, Rug Sirdar Hayfield Bonus Chunky yarns: Wheat (816) = 250 g and Black (965) = 5 g
- 6.00 mm hook.
- Polyester fibrefill 600 g
- 15 mm safety eyes
- Tapestry needle
- Pins

For body only (without feet) use:

- Sirdar Hayfield Bonus Chunky yarns: Wheat (816) = 190 g and Black (965) = 5 g
- Polyester fibrefill 450 g

Body

With color Wheat (816), follow the instructions of Body Pattern on page 52.

Feet

Make 2 feet in Wheat (816) color, follow the Feet Pattern on page 53.

Ear

Make 2 in Wheat (816) color.
Rnd 1: Ch 2, 6 sc in second chain from hook. (6)
Rnd 2: 2 sc in each st around. (12)
Rnd 3: (Sc in next st, 2 sc in next st) around. (18)
Rnd 4: (2 sc in next st, sc in next 2 sts) around. (24)
Rnd 5: (Sc in next 3 sts, 2 sc in next st) around. (30)
Rnd 6-8: Sc in each st around. (30)
Rnd 9: (Sc next 2 sts tog, sc in next 3 sts) around. (24)
Row 10: Working in row, flatten last rnd, matching sts and working through both thicknesses, sc in next 11 sts, leave long end for sewing, fasten off. (11)

Finishing

Pin ears on rnds 21-31 and sew. With Black yarn embroider nose as in picture.

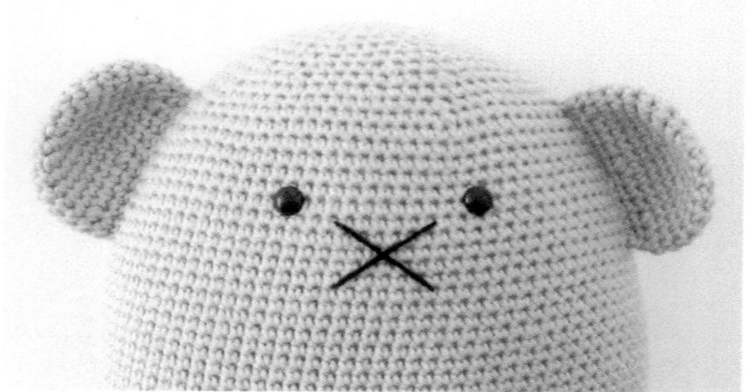

Owl

Material

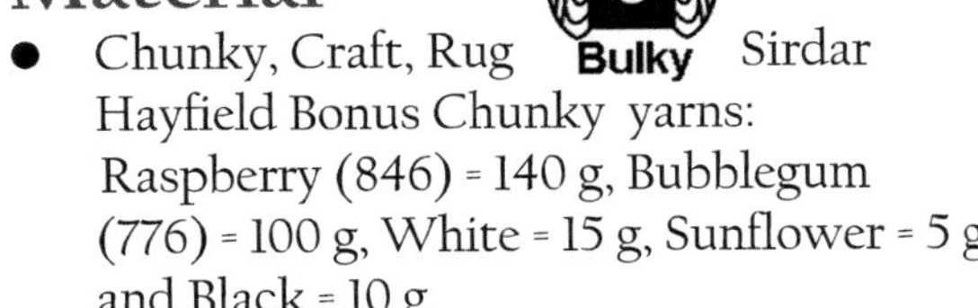

- Chunky, Craft, Rug Sirdar Hayfield Bonus Chunky yarns: Raspberry (846) = 140 g, Bubblegum (776) = 100 g, White = 15 g, Sunflower = 5 g and Black = 10 g
- 6.00 mm hook.
- Polyester fibrefill 600 g
- Tapestry needle.
- Pins

For body only (without feet) use:

- Sirdar Hayfield Bonus Chunky yarns: Raspberry (846) = 80 g, Bubblegum (776) = 100 g, White = 15 g, Sunflower = 5 g and Black = 10 g
- Polyester fibrefill 450 g

Body

Follow the instructions of Body Pattern on page 52.

Rnd 1-18: color Raspberry (846).
Rnd 19-42: color Bubblegum (776).

Feet

Make 2 feet in Raspberry (846) color, follow the Feet Pattern on page 53.

Ear

Make 2 in Bubblegum (776) color.
Rnd 1: Ch 2, 6 sc in second chain from hook. (6)
Rnd 2: (Sc in next st, 2 sc in next st) around. (9)
Rnd 3: (2 sc in next st, sc in next 2 sts) around. (12)
Rnd 4: (Sc in next 3 sts, 2 sc in next st) around. (15)
Rnd 5: Sc in next 2 sts, 2 sc in next st, (sc in next 4 sts, 2 sc in next st) 2 times, sc in next 2 sts. (18)
Rnd 6: (Sc in next 5 sts, 2 sc in next st) around, join with sl st in first st. Leave long end for sewing, fasten off. (21)
Sew the opening of ear close flat.

Eye

White color, make 2
Rnd 1: Ch 2, 6 sc in second chain from hook. (6)
Rnd 2: 2 sc in each st around. (12)
Rnd 3: (Sc in next st, 2 sc in next st) around. (18)
Rnd 4: (2 sc in next st, sc in next 2 sts) around. (24)
Rnd 5: (Sc in next 3 sts, 2 sc in next st) around. (30)
Rnd 6: Sc in next 2 sts, 2 sc in next st, (sc in next 4 sts, 2 sc in next st) 5 times, sc in next 2 sts. (36)
Rnd 7: (Sc in next 5 sts, 2 sc in next st) around, join with sl st in first st, leave long end for sewing, fasten off. (42)

Black color, make 2
Rnd 1: Ch 2, 6 sc in second chain from hook. (6)
Rnd 2: 2 sc in each st around. (12)
Rnd 3: (Sc in next st, 2 sc in next st) around, join with sl st in first st, leave long end for sewing, fasten off. (18)
Sew the black eyes on middle of the white eyes.

Beak

Rnd 1: With Yellow (Sunflower), ch 2, 6 sc in second chain from hook. (6)
Rnd 2: (Sc in next st, 2 sc in next st) around. (9)
Rnd 3: Sc in each st around. (9)
Rnd 4: (2 sc in next st, sc in next 2 sts) around. (12)
Rnd 5: (Sc in next 3 sts, 2 sc in next st) around. (15)
Rnd 6: Sc in next 2 sts, 2 sc in next st, (sc in next 4 sts, 2 sc in next st) 2 times, sc in next 2 sts. (18)
Row 7: Working in row, flatten last rnd, matching sts and working through both thicknesses, sc in next 8 sts, leave long end for sewing, fasten off. (8)

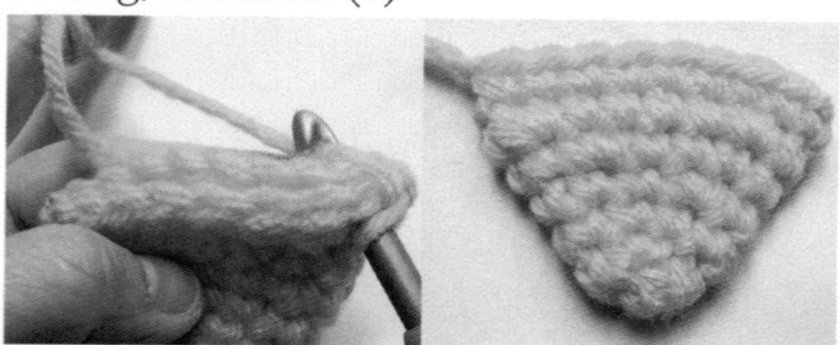

Finishing

Pin ears on rnds 28-35 and sew. Pin eyes on rnds 19-30 and sew. Sew beak in the middle between eyes on rnds 19-20.

Ducky

Material

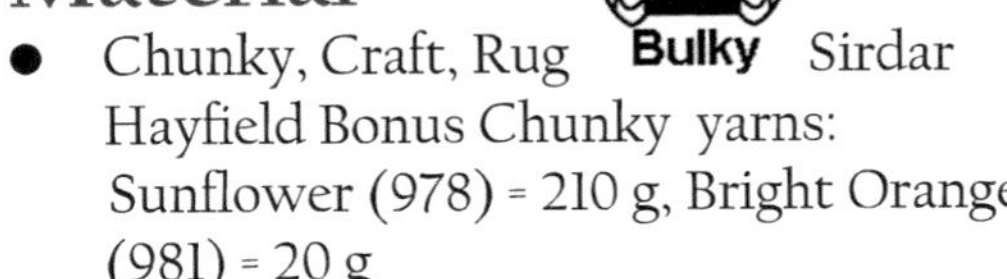

- Chunky, Craft, Rug Sirdar Hayfield Bonus Chunky yarns: Sunflower (978) = 210 g, Bright Orange (981) = 20 g
- 6.00 mm hook.
- Polyester fibrefill 600 g
- 15 mm safety eyes
- Tapestry needle.
- Pins

For body only (without feet) use:

- Sirdar Hayfield Bonus Chunky yarns: Sunflower (978) = 150 g, Bright Orange (981) = 20 g
- Polyester fibrefill 450 g

Body

With color Sunflower (978), follow the instructions of Body Pattern on page 52.

Feet

Make 2 feet in Sunflower (978) color, follow the Feet Pattern on page 53.

Beak

Make 2 in Bright Orange (981) color.

Rnd 1: Ch 11, sc in second chain from hook, sc in next 8 chs, 3 sc in last ch; working in remaining loops on opposite side of chain, sc in next 8 chs, 2 sc in next ch. (22)

x x x x x x x x x x o
x o o o o o o o o o o x
x x x x x x x x x x

o = chain x = sc

Rnd 2: 2 sc in next st, sc in next 8 sts, 2 sc in next 3 sts, sc in next 8 sts, 2 sc in next 2 sts. (28)
Rnd 3-5: Sc in each st around. (28)
Rnd 6: (Sc in next 5 sts, sc next 2 sts tog) around. (24)
Rnd 7: Sc in each st around. (24)
Row 8: Working in row, flatten last rnd, matching sts and working through both thicknesses, sc in next 9 sts, fasten off. (9)

Joining the last row of the 2 pieces together, you can sew the last rows together or join them with single crochet stitches.

This is how to join 2 pieces with single crochet stitches: hold 2 pieces together, with Bright Orange (981) crochet sc through the last row of both pieces across, leave long end for sewing, fasten off. (9)

Finishing

Sew the last round of beak on rnd 24.

Hair on top: Cut 20 pieces of yellow yarn (Sunflower 978) 4" (10 cm) long. Hold one strand of yarn, fold in half, insert hook through a stitch on middle top of head, draw the folded end through the stitch and pull the loose ends through the folded end, draw the knot up tightly. Add 19 more hairs.

Use needle or comb/ hair brush to split the yarns to make them look fluffy.

Froggy

Material

- Chunky, Craft, Rug 5 Bulky Sirdar Hayfield Bonus Chunky yarns: Bright Green (886) = 230 g, White (961) = 10 g and Black (965) = 5 g
- 6.00 mm hook.
- Polyester fibrefill 600 g
- Two of 25 mm Black buttons for eyes
- Tapestry needle.
- Pins

For body only (without feet) use:

- Sirdar Hayfield Bonus Chunky yarns: Bright Green (886) = 170 g, White (961) = 10 g and Black (965) = 5 g
- Polyester fibrefill 450 g

Body

With color Bright Green (886), follow the instructions of Body Pattern on page 52.

Feet

Make 2 in Bright Green (886) color, follow the Feet Pattern on page 53.

Eye

White color, make 2

Rnd 1: Ch 2, 6 sc in second chain from hook. (6)
Rnd 2: 2 sc in each st around. (12)
Rnd 3: (Sc in next st, 2 sc in next st) around. (18)
Rnd 4: (2 sc in next st, sc in next 5 sts) around. (21)
Rnd 5-7: Sc in each st around. (21)
Rnd 8: (Sc in next 5 sts, sc next 2 sts tog) around. (18)
Rnd 9: (Sc in next st, sc next 2 sts tog) around, join with sl st in first st, leave long end for sewing, fasten off. (12)

Sew button on middle top of White eye and stuff.

Bright Green (886) color, make 2

Rnd 1: Ch 2, 6 sc in second chain from hook. (6)
Rnd 2: 2 sc in each st around. (12)
Rnd 3: (Sc in next st, 2 sc in next st) around. (18)
Rnd 4: (2 sc in next st, sc in next 2 sts) around. (24)
Rnd 5-6: Sc in each st around. (24)
Rnd 7: Sc in each st around, join with sl st in first st, leave long end for sewing, fasten off. (24)

Put the white eye inside the green eye and sew (see picture).

Finishing

Sew eyes on rnds 35-37. With Black yarn embroider mouth 7 sts apart on rnds 30-33 as in picture.

Cat

Material

- Chunky, Craft, Rug Sirdar Hayfield Bonus Chunky yarns: Cinder (786) = 250 g and Black (965) = 5 g
- 6.0 mm hook.
- Polyester fibrefill 600 g
- 15 mm safety eyes
- Tapestry needle.
- Pins

For body only (without feet) use:

- Sirdar Hayfield Bonus Chunky yarns: Cinder (786) = 190 g and Black (965) = 5 g
- Polyester fibrefill 450 g

Body

With color Cinder (786), follow the instructions of Body Pattern on page 52.

Feet

Make 2 feet in Cinder (786) color, follow the Feet Pattern on page 53.

Ear

Make 2 in Cinder (786) color.

Rnd 1: Ch 2, 6 sc in second chain from hook. (6)
Rnd 2: (Sc in next st, 2 sc in next st) around. (9)
Rnd 3: (2 sc in next st, sc in next 2 sts) around. (12)
Rnd 4: (Sc in next 3 sts, 2 sc in next st) around. (15)
Rnd 5: (2 sc in next st, sc in next 4 sts) around. (18)
Rnd 6: (Sc in next 5 sts, 2 sc in next st) around. (21)
Rnd 7: (2 sc in next st, sc in next 6 sts) around. (24)
Rnd 8: Sc in each st around. (24)
Rnd 9: (Sc next 2 sts tog, sc in next 2 sts) around, join with sl st in first st, leave long end for sewing, fasten off. (18)

Finishing

Pin ears on rnds 25-34 and sew. With Black yarn embroider nose as in picture.

Bunny

Material

- Chunky, Craft, Rug (5 Bulky) Sirdar Hayfield Bonus Chunky yarns: Mint (956) = 280 g and Black (965) = 5 g
- 6.0 mm hook.
- Polyester fibrefill 600 g
- 15 mm safety eyes
- Tapestry needle.
- Pins

For body only (without feet) use:

- Sirdar Hayfield Bonus Chunky yarns: Mint (956) = 220 g and Black (965) = 5 g
- Polyester fibrefill 450 g

Body

With color Mint (956), follow the instructions of Body Pattern on page 52.

Feet

Make 2 feet in Mint (956) color, follow the Feet pattern on page 53.

Ear

Make 2 in Mint (956) color.

Rnd 1: Ch 11, sc in second chain from hook, sc in next 8 chs, 3 sc in last ch; working in remaining loops on opposite side of chain, sc in next 8 chs, 2 sc in next ch. (22)

```
   x  x  x  x  x  x  x  x  x  x  o
x  o  o  o  o  o  o  o  o  o  o  x
   x  x  x  x  x  x  x  x  x  x
```

o = chain   x = sc

Rnd 2: 2 sc in next st, sc in next 8 sts, 2 sc in next 3 sts, sc in next 8 sts, 2 sc in next 2 sts. (28)
Rnd 3: Sc in next st, 2 sc in next st, sc in next 9 sts, (2 sc in next st, sc in next st) 2 times, 2 sc in next st, sc in next 9 sts, 2 sc in next st, sc in next st, 2 sc in next st. (34)
Rnd 4: Sc in each st around. (34)
Rnd 5: 2 sc in next st, sc in next 10 sts, 2 sc in next st, (sc in next 2 sts, 2 sc in next st) 2 times, sc in next 10 sts, (2 sc in next st, sc in next 2 sts) 2 times. (40)
Rnd 6-8: Sc in each st around. (40)
Rnd 9: Sc in next 3 sts, sc next 2 sts tog, (sc in next 6 sts, sc next 2 sts tog) 4 times, sc in next 3 sts. (35)
Rnd 10: Sc in each st around. (35)
Rnd 11: (Sc in next 5 sts, sc next 2 sts tog) around. (30)
Rnd 12: Sc in each st around. (30)
Rnd 13: Sc in next 2 sts, sc next 2 sts tog, (sc in next 4 sts, sc next 2 sts tog) 4 times, sc in next 2 sts. (25)
Rnd 14: Sc in each st around. (25)
Rnd 15: (Sc in next 3 sts, sc next 2 sts tog) around. (20)
Rnd 16: Sc in each st around. (20)
Rnd 17: (Sc in next 2 sts, sc next 2 sts tog) around. (15)
Rnd 18: Sc in each st around. (15)
Rnd 19: (Sc in next st, sc next 2 sts tog) around. (10)
Rnd 20: Sc in each st around, join with sl st in first st, leave long end for sewing, fasten off. (10)

Fold ear in half and sew.

Hold 2 ears together and sew the end of ears together, then sew side of ears together about 4 rounds.

Finishing

Sew ears on middle top of head and sew both side of ears on rnds 38-42. With Black yarn embroider nose as in picture.

How to join Yarn.

Join yarn to free loop, ch 1, sc in same st.

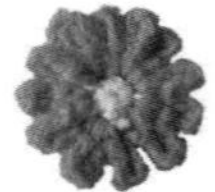

How to read pattern.

Rnd 4: (Sc in next 2 sts, 2 sc in next st) around. (24)
Number (24) at the end of round = number of stitches after finished round.

Rnd 5: (Sc in next 3 sts, 2 sc in next st) around. (30)
Repeat (Sc in next 3 sts, 2 sc in next st) until end of round
=> **Rnd 5:** (Sc in next 3 sts, 2 sc in next st), (Sc in next 3 sts, 2 sc in next st), (Sc in next 3 sts, 2 sc in next st), (Sc in next 3 sts, 2 sc in next st), (Sc in next 3 sts, 2 sc in next st), (Sc in next 3 sts, 2 sc in next st)
Total stitches of Rnd 5 = 5+5+5+5+5+5 = 30 sts

Rnd 6: Sc in next 2 sts, 2 sc in next st, (sc in next 4 sts, 2 sc in next st) 5 times, sc in next 2 sts. (36)
Repeat (sc in next 4 sts, 2 sc in next st) 5 times
=> **Rnd 6:** Sc in next 2 sts, 2 sc in next st, (sc in next 4 sts, 2 sc in next st), (sc in next 4 sts, 2 sc in next st), (sc in next 4 sts, 2 sc in next st), (sc in next 4 sts, 2 sc in next st), (sc in next 4 sts, 2 sc in next st), sc in next 2 sts.
Total stitches of Rnd 6 = 2+2+6+6+6+6+6+2 = 36 sts

Yarn Weight System				
USA		UK	Australia	Recommended Hook in Metric (mm)
0 Lace	Lace weight	1 ply	2 ply	1.5 - 2.25 mm
1 Super fine	Fingering	2 ply	3 ply	2.25 - 3 mm
	Sock	3 ply	3 ply	2.25 - 3.5 mm
2 Fine	Sport	4 ply	5 ply	3.5 - 4.5 mm
3 Light	DK Light worsted	DK	8 ply	4.5 - 5.5 mm
4 Medium	Worsted	Aran	10 ply	5.5 - 6.5 mm
5 Bulky	Bulky	Chunky	12 ply	6.5 - 9 mm
6 Super Bulky	Super Bulky	Super Chunky	14 ply	9 mm and larger

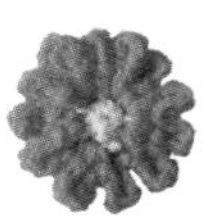

Crochet Hook Size Conversion			
Hook in Metric (mm)	USA	UK	Japanese
1.00 mm	10 steel	4 steel	4 steel
1.25 mm	8 steel	3 steel	2 steel
1.50 mm	7 steel	2.5 steel	--
1.75 mm	4 steel	2 steel	--
2.00 mm	--	14	2/0
2.25 mm	B/1	13	3/0
2.50 mm	--	12	4/0
2.75 mm	C/2	--	--
3.00 mm	--	11	5/0
3.25 mm	D/3	10	--
3.50 mm	E/4	9	6/0
3.75 mm	F/5	--	--
4.00 mm	G/6	8	7/0
4.50 mm	7	7	7.5/0
5.00 mm	H/8	6	8/0
5.50 mm	I/9	5	--
6.00 mm	J/10	4	10/0
6.50 mm	K/10.5	3	7
7.00 mm	--	2	--
8.00 mm	L/11	0	8
9.00 mm	M/13	00	9
10.00 mm	N/15	000	10

Copyright

First Edition
Date of publication: July 14th 2014
Publisher:
K and J Publishing
Cambridge, England

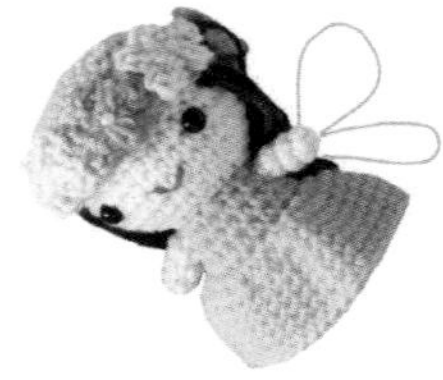

16062196R10045

Printed in Poland
by Amazon Fulfillment
Poland Sp. z o.o., Wrocław